FERRY TALES

Tyne-Norway Voyages 1864-2001

Dick Keys and Ken Smith

Tyne Bridge Publishing

Newcastle Libraries & Information Service

Acknowledgements:

The authors wish to thank the following for their generous help: Ged Henderson, Editor of *The Journal*, Newcastle, for permission to use photographs from the library of Newcastle Chronicle and Journal Ltd; Dag Romslo, Fjord Line; Joyce Hall, Tynemouth; David Robertson, Newcastle; Martin Melling, Cleadon; Ann Jobling, South Shields; Olga Carlson, South Shields; Kari Thúróczy, Oslo; Rigmor Grimsø, Husøysund; Joe Addison, South Shields; Joan Phillips, Cullercoats; Pat Fawcett, Whitley Bay; Alan Chaplin, Wallsend; Nick Robinson, Seaton Sluice; Michael Irwin, Newcastle; John Winterburn, Dumfries; Bill Laverty, Prudhoe; Albert Bulley, South Shields; Gordon Kell, Gateshead; Mike Shipley, Newbiggin; Mr R. Walker, Kendal; Peter Pennock, South Shields; John Dobson, Newcastle; Ron French, Wooler; and the staff of Newcastle Libraries & Information Service.

Published by City of Newcastle upon Tyne Education & Libraries Directorate
Newcastle Libraries & Information Service
Tyne Bridge Publishing, 2002

ISBN: 1857951514

Printed by Elanders Hindson, UK

Cover photograph: *Venus* arrives at the Tyne Commission Quay, 1937 (for details see page 20), reproduced courtesy of Newcastle Chronicle and Journal Ltd.

A selection of further maritime publications from Tyne Bridge Publishing at Newcastle Libraries & Information Service:

By Dick Keys and Ken Smith:

Down Elswick Slipways: Armstrong's Ships and People 1884-1918.

From Walker to the World: Charles Mitchell's Low Walker Shipyard.

Black Diamonds by Sea: North-East Sailing Colliers 1780-1880.

Steamers at the Staiths: Steam Colliers of the North-East 1841-1945.

By Ian Rae and Ken Smith:

Swan Hunter: the Pride and the Tears.

By Ken Smith:

Turbinia: the Story of Charles Parsons and his Ocean Greyhound.

Mauretania: Pride of the Tyne.

From Tyne to Titanic: the Story of Rescue Ship Carpathia.

Books, and free catalogue, available from:
Tyne Bridge Publishing, City Library, Princess Square, Newcastle upon Tyne NE99 1DX.

Find Tyne Bridge Publishing on the web at www.newcastle.gov.uk/tynebridgepublishing

Contents

Illustrations

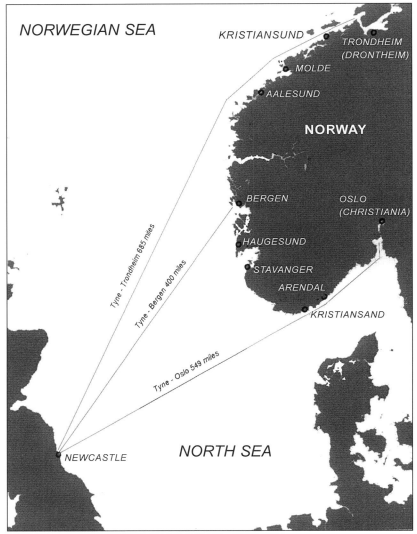

*Left: The first **Jupiter** approaches the Tyne Commission Quay, North Shields, in 1948. She entered service on the Newcastle run during the First World War in 1916, but the following year was withdrawn from service because of the intensified U-boat campaign. She survived both World Wars, and was a familiar sight in the Tyne for many years.*

Right: A map showing the sea routes to Trondheim, Bergen and Oslo.

~ Forging the Links ~

The links between the North-East of England and Norway have been strong and long-lasting ones. Friendship, business, pleasure and wartime ordeals have all featured in the story of these close ties.

Norwegians, along with other Scandinavians, regularly visit Tyneside to shop at Newcastle's Eldon Square and the MetroCentre in Gateshead. Many Tynesiders have also visited Norway and marvelled at its majestic and awesome scenery. Often they travel by sea, embarking and disembarking at the Tyne Commission Quay, North Shields. The Tyne sea route is the shortest between England and the land of the fjords. Even today, despite aircraft, it remains important.

Looking back, it can be seen that the advent of the steamship on the North Sea in the 1860s was a major first step in establishing fast, reliable and regular voyages between the two areas and forging those warm, friendly links.

It was coal which began it all. On March 4 1864 the steamship *Baron Hambro* sailed from Newcastle bound for Trondheim in Norway with 106 tons of coal and 25 tons of pig iron. The vessel had been chartered by shipping agents A.C. Houen & Co., of the Quayside, Newcastle. The *Baron Hambro*, commanded by a Captain Bryant, thus began one of the earliest recorded steamer services from the Tyne to Norway. The ship evidently made it back safely to Newcastle, for 20 days later she again sailed from the river for Trondheim, this time with a much more diverse cargo which included paints, roll sulphur, cheese, peas, tools, earthenware, biscuits, grindstones, hammer heads, flint

In this 1864 advertisement Trondheim is spelled Drontheim, a spelling common at this period.

glass, twine, seeds, alkali, soap and bar and bolt iron. Also being carried was the lifeblood of the Tyne, coal.

By April the *Baron Hambro* had been joined on the Trondheim run, for one or two voyages, by another steamer, the Tyne-owned *Chipchase*, under the command of a Captain Wallis.

In 1865 A.C. Houen & Co declared in an advertisement in the *Newcastle upon Tyne Bill of Entry and Shipping List* that "the fine new screw steamer *Hilda* … is intended to be dispatched for Trondheim on or about the 11th August". In all, the *Hilda* made about four voyages to Norway during that year. A few passengers may have been carried on this vessel and the two earlier ones.

The 1860s also saw other shipping agents chartering steamers for the Tyne-Norway trade. They included Fedden Brothers, William Southern, and Borries Craig &

Co, all of which had offices in the Quayside area of Newcastle.

The first mention of a passenger service on a steamship from Newcastle to Norway seems to have been on April 27 1865 when Fedden Brothers announced in an advertisement that the new, first-class, steamer *Nordland*, commanded by Captain D. Lysholm, was to sail from Newcastle on or about May 20 for Trondheim with a call at Bergen on the way.

The advertisement, headed "Direct Steam Communication Between Newcastle and the North of Norway", informed potential travellers that the *Nordland* "offers a most favourable opportunity to tourists, having very superior accommodation for about 60 first-class passengers". The ship had been built on the Tyne by John Wigham Richardson's Neptune Yard at Low Walker, Newcastle. She was among the first of many Tyne-Norway

DIRECT STEAM COMMUNICATION BETWEEN NEWCASTLE and the NORTH of NORWAY.

THE new First-class Steamer "NORDLAND," built under special survey, and commanded by Capt. D. Lysholm, is appointed to sail from Newcastle, on or about the 20th May, for Drontheim, calling at Bergen.

This Steamer offers a most favourable opportunity to Tourists, having very superior Accomodation for about Sixty first-class Passengers.

Goods and Passengers also taken to intermediate Ports between Drontheim and Bergen; and Goods only, to other Ports on the West Coast of Norway.

For Rates of Freight and Passage, apply to
FEDDEN BROTHERS,
Newcastle-on-Tyne.

27 April 1865

steamers to be built in the shipyards of North-East England.

In July 1865, another shipping agent, William Southern, of Custom House Building, Quayside, Newcastle, announced in the *Newcastle upon Tyne Bill of Entry and Shipping List* the beginning of a "regular"

REGULAR STEAM COMMUNICATION TO NORWAY.

THE first-class Steamer "QUEEN," 500 Tons, will leave the Tyne, on or about the 14th July, for DRONTHEIM, calling at Aalesund, Molde, and Christiansund, returning, *via* same route, to Newcastle-on-Tyne, and will continue on this line during the season.

First-class accommodation for Passengers.

For Freight, &c., apply to WILLIAM SOUTHERN, Quayside, Newcastle.

6 July 1865

steamship service to Norway. This was the first use of the word "regular" in any advertisement for the route.

The advertisement declared that the first-class steamer *Queen* would sail for Trondheim later that month, making calls at Aalesund, Molde and Christiansund on the way. The vessel would return by the same route and would continue such sailings throughout the rest of the summer season. The *Queen* left Newcastle on July 17 with a varied cargo, including, of course, coal.

In July 1868 Borries Craig & Co., of Newcastle, advertised that the new Norwegian steamer *Saga*, commanded by a Captain Wulf, was to sail from Newcastle to Bergen and would continue such sailings every fortnight during the rest of the summer season. Passengers were carried in this ship as well as freight. She appears to have made about nine crossings during 1868. The *Saga* had been built on the Tyne at Wigham Richardson's Neptune Yard.

The *Saga* was still sailing to Bergen in 1870, taking passengers, coal and general cargo out to Bergen and returning to Newcastle with sulphur pirites and sulphur ore. In June of that year another vessel chartered by Borries Craig joined the route. She was the new steamer *Odin*, which was stated to have "first rate accommodation for passengers". Captain Wulf left the *Saga* to take command of the *Odin*. His place aboard the *Saga* was taken by a Captain Kahas. The *Odin* had been built on the Tees at Middlesbrough.

The year 1870 also saw the famous transatlantic shipping company, the Allan Line of Liverpool and Glasgow, begin sailings between the Tyne and Norway. It began fortnightly voyages from the river to Trondheim where its

> ALLAN LINE.
>
> DIRECT STEAM COMMUNICATION
> BETWEEN
> ## TYNE AND NORWAY.
> THE Fine Iron Screw Steamer "NORWAY," 1000 tons, will sail from TYNE TO DRONTHEIM, on 15th April, and every Fortnight thereafter, during the Season, and affords a good opportunity for shipment of Goods. This Steamer has also first-rate accommodation for Cabin Passengers.
> Apply to ALLAN BROTHERS & Co., Liverpool;
> or to
> JAMES BLACK & Co., 2, Lombard Street,
> Newcastle-upon-Tyne
>
> BERGEN is a port of call on the Homeward Voyage, on 9th of April, and every alternate Saturday thereafter.
>
> *14 May 1870*

ship, the *Norway*, would pick up immigrants and other travellers bound for Canada and the USA.

The main function of the *Norway* was to serve as a "feeder" vessel to the Allan Line's transatlantic passenger services between Liverpool and Glasgow and the ports of North America. After landing on Tyneside, the Norwegian immigrants were taken to Liverpool and Glasgow by train from Newcastle. The last of the Allan Line's runs to and from Norway were made in 1872.

In the spring of 1871 the newly-formed Norse

American Line, whose agents on the Tyne were Borries Craig, began a steamer service from the Tyne to New York, with a call at Bergen for immigrants. Their ship, the *St Olaf*, had been completed by Wigham Richardson's Neptune Yard earlier that year. The *St Olaf* was the pioneer vessel of the Norse American Line and this sailing to New York was the first made by the company.

In spring 1873 the *St Olaf* was still sailing from the Tyne to New York, making calls at Christiana (Oslo) and

> ### TYNE TO BERGEN.
> TAKING GOODS FOR ALL PORTS NORTH AND SOUTH OF BERGEN.
> STEAMER................."SAGA"...sailing about 18th March.
> DO. ...."ODIN"... ,, 22nd March.
> For Freight and Passage, apply to
> BORRIES, CRAIG, & Co., Lombard Street.
>
> NORSE AMERICAN LINE OF STEAMSHIPS.
> TYNE TO NEW YORK, CALLING AT CHRISTIANIA AND BERGEN FOR EMIGRANTS.
> STEAMER................."ST. OLAF" ......sailing 20th March.
> DO. ...."FRITHIOF" .... ,, 1st April.
> DO. ...."HAKON ADELSTEN"... ,, 17th April.
> For Freight and full Particulars, apply to
> BORRIES, CRAIG, & Co., Lombard Street, Newcastle.
>
> . TYNE TO CHRISTIANIA.
> Taking Goods for all neighbouring Ports.
> STEAMER................."ST. OLAF"...sailing about 20th March.
> For Freight and Particulars, apply to
> BORRIES, CRAIG, & Co., Lombard Street.
>
> REGULAR LINE OF STEAMERS FROM THE TYNE TO CHRISTIANSAND, ARENDAL, & CHRISTIANIA, TAKING GOODS FOR THE NEIGHBOURING PORTS.
> THE S.S. "THULE" will commence to Load on or about the 31st inst., Sailing on or about the 1st April.
> For Particulars, apply to
> C. HASSELL,
> Exchange Buildings, Newcastle-upon-Tyne.
>
> ### TYNE TO DRONTHEIM, &c.
> ON or about the 10th April, the Norwegian Royal Mail Steamer "NORDLAND," Capt. A. O, Berg, will be despatched to Drontheim, taking Goods for all Ports between that place and Vadsø. Excellent accommodation for Passengers.
> For rates of Freight and Passage, apply to
> PEDDEN BROTHERS & Co.,
> 2, Queen Street, Newcastle-on-Tyne.
>
> *22 March 1873*

sometimes Bergen. Later that year she was joined on the route by three other ships, the *Hakon Adelsten*, the *Kong Sverre* and the *Peter Jebsen*.

William Southern, Fedden Brothers and Borries Craig continued to operate steamships on the runs to Norway during the 1870s, with Christiana and Stavanger featuring among the ports as well as Bergen and Trondheim. Other firms which made forays into the trade included the Wilson Line, of Hull, and Cory Brothers, who had offices in Newcastle.

In February 1878 Borries Craig advertised fortnightly sailings to Bergen using the *Nordlyset*, commanded by a Captain Bjelek. In May the *Vigsnaes*, under Captain Romsloe, made an appearance in the advertisements and in September the *Odin*, commanded by Captain Zeisler. These ships were offering a "passengers only" service.

North Shields c.1880.

On February 16 1880 Cory Brothers advertised that the steamship *Carlotta* would run regularly between the Tyne and Bergen. An advertisement on June 15 stated that the "fine new steamer *Carlotta* (Captain Lund) will sail on Tuesday on or about every fortnight for Bergen. Splendid accommodation for passengers. Fare, including board, £2.10s."

Steamships carrying passengers between the Tyne and Norway were therefore, by the 1880s, an established part of the river's busy life.

~ Passengers and Mail ~

During all these developments another shipping business, the Bergen Steamship Company (in Norwegian, Det Bergenske Dampskibsselskab), also known as the Bergen Line, had been operating a steamer service between Bergen and Hamburg. One of this Norwegian company's officials was Peter Gabriel Halvorsen who was to play a pioneer role in developing the Tyne service.

Halvorsen eventually left the Bergen Line and in 1871 took the initiative of setting up his own shipping business to import coal from Britain to Norway. It bore the appropriate name "Coal Company of 1871".

Within a few years Halvorsen had realised the potential of the passenger trade. In 1879 he began using vessels on a regular weekly service from the Tyne to Bergen, with passengers being carried as well as cargo. The following year a new ship was delivered to his company, the *Johan Sverdrup*, and placed on these weekly sailings. In 1882 she was joined by another vessel, the *Norge*.

Halvorsen clearly wished to expand the passenger trade to meet growing demand and he knew that he might be able to obtain a Norwegian government subsidy if his ships also undertook to carry the mails. In 1886-87 he applied for such a subsidy, but was turned down.

However, Peter Halvorsen's company was not the only one keen to carry mail and passengers on the route between the Tyne and western Norway. In 1888, about a year after Halvorsen's unsuccessful application, the Bergen Line, in co-operation with the Northern Steamship Company (Nordenfjeldske) of Trondheim, applied to the

Gordon Kell

*Built at Sunderland, the Bergen Line's first **Vega** in dry dock, 1895. She was launched by J.L. Thompson & Son at Sunderland in 1895. The **Vega** was to be sunk by a U-boat in 1916. Note the Bergen Line stars on the bows.*

*An advertisement from the Royal Mining Engineering and Industrial Exhibition Catalogue, 1887. The **Norge** entered service in 1882 on the North Sea run.*

Norwegian government for a contract and subsidy to carry the mails.

Eventually it was agreed, with the approval of the country's parliament, the Storthing, that the Bergen Line, the Northern Steamship Company and Halvorsen's business would operate a joint mail and passenger service between Newcastle, Bergen and Trondheim.

The new, shared service began on May 31 1890 when the Bergen Line's *Mercur* sailed from her home port for the Tyne.

Halvorsen operated two round voyages a week on the Bergen-Newcastle run, with calls at Stavanger. His steamers left the Albert Edward Dock at North Shields every Wednesday at 7pm and every Saturday at 7pm. A single fare was £3 and a return £5. A passage in the *Norge* to Bergen was advertised as taking 36 hours.

The Bergen Line and Northern Steamship Company shared a once-a-week round voyage service on the Trondheim-Bergen-Newcastle route. Their ships left the Albert Edward Dock every Tuesday at 7pm for Bergen, Aalesund, Molde, Christiansund and Trondheim. The shared service was to become known as the B & N Line.

The Northern Steamship Company chose a newly completed ship for the route, the *Ragnvald Jarl*, which had been launched at Wigham Richardson's Neptune Yard in early 1890. By this date the yard had gained a reputation for providing soundly-built Norwegian steamers. The *Ragnvald Jarl* served for many years, but was taken off the route in 1907 and replaced by the Trondheim-built *Haakon VII*.

Halvorsen also ordered a new steamer for his part in the route. He is said to have designed the ship himself. However, this vessel, the clipper-bowed *Britannia*, was not a success and became unpopular with passengers because of too much vibration and rolling. These flaws, together with the loss of his other ship, the *Norge*, hit Halvorsen's business so badly that his company collapsed in 1892. The *Norge*, commanded by a Captain Jacobsen, ran aground near Tynanger, off Stavanger, in December 1891. The passengers, crew and mails were all saved.

It was around this time that the Bergen Line had acquired its own new ship, the *Venus*. She was built by C.S. Swan & Hunter at their Wallsend Yard on the Tyne, being completed in 1890 and entering service on the route in 1893. Her triple expansion engines were supplied by the Wallsend Slipway & Engineering Company. The ship was to have a long and successful career and was not broken up until 1933.

The *Venus*, the first Bergen Line ship to bear the name

of the planet, was launched in February 1890 and was described by the *Newcastle Daily Journal* as a "smart looking steel screw steamer". It became a tradition for the Bergen company's vessels to be named after stars or planets and for many years they carried the emblem of a star on their bows.

In 1895 a sister ship for the run, the *Vega*, was completed at the River Wear yard of J.L. Thompson & Sons, Sunderland. A third steamer, the *Irma*, began sailings on the route in 1905. *Irma* had also been launched in North-East England, being completed by Sir Raylton Dixon & Co., at Middlesbrough on the River Tees.

Ships launched in the North-East of England were thus linking the region of their birth with western Norway.

*Men on the stern of the **Vega** in dock.*

*The starboard side of the first **Vega's** fo'c'sle. The sails are brailed to the mast and furled on the forestay. A steam winch can be seen, bottom left.*

~ Perils of War ~

As well as the run to Bergen and Trondheim, a passenger ship service also developed linking Norway's capital city, Christiana (later renamed Oslo), with the Tyne.

In 1890 the East Norway Lloyd Line (Det Ostlandske Lloyd) began a passenger service between Newcastle and Christiana via Arendal and Larvik. The line had previously used cargo ships on the route and these carried some passengers.

The first ship on the new service was the *Stirling*. She was later joined by the *Sovereign*. The single first-class fare to and from Oslo was £2.10s, with a return fare costing £4. A second-class single was £1.10s and a return £2.10s. The passage to Oslo at this date was usually around 65 hours.

In 1906, however, Fred Olsen Line, of Oslo, took over this service from East Norway Lloyd. Olsen, one of the best known names in Norwegian shipping, thus began a long-lasting link with the Tyne.

Fred Olsen replaced the old *Stirling* with a new ship of the same name, and in 1912 the *Sovereign* was replaced with the *Bessheim*.

The outbreak of the First World War in 1914 did not bring immediate suspension of the steamers to and from Bergen, although the Northern Steamship Company ceased its sailings with *Haakon VII*, resuming them later for a short time. For the first two years of the conflict no ships of either the Bergen or Fred Olsen lines were sunk.

However, on November 16 1916 the *Vega* was sent to the bottom by a U-boat while on passage from her home port to Newcastle. The attack took place about 20 miles off western Norway's Joederan Reef. The *Vega* was sunk by a torpedo and shells.

Fortunately, the 16 passengers and 32 crew managed to board lifeboats and were rescued by the steamer *Columbia* of the Danish East Asiatic Line. The ship landed them safely at Stavanger. Among those in the lifeboats were two diplomats on their way to join the Swedish Mission in London.

The *Vega* had been stopped on two previous occasions by German submarines but had been allowed to continue after being told to throw her cargo overboard.

In the incident which led to her loss, the U-boat commander ordered the *Vega* to be sunk after discovering she was carrying food to Britain. The Germans were clearly intensifying their campaign of war.

It was reported that she had on board a cargo consisting of 110 tons of canned food and registered mail to the value of £40,000. But a later account stated that she had been carrying machinery and the Germans had refused to wait for it to be thrown overboard. A rumour arose that the attack was due to espionage at Stavanger.

Whatever the truth of the matter, the managing director of the Bergen Line, Kristofer Lehmkuhl, said the *Vega* was only loaded with one fifth of her possible cargo.

The line now suspended its regular passenger ship services to Britain. Despite this, in March 1917 the *Venus* was sent on a voyage to Newcastle to see if it might be feasible to resume regular passenger sailings. She managed to

*The Norway Wharf of the Bergen and Northern Steamship Line's joint service at Newcastle Quayside, c. 1914-15. Alongside is Bergen's **Capella**, which may have been on relief duties. Ferries were to sail to Bergen from this wharf until 1928 when the Tyne Commission Quay, also known as the Riverside Quay, at North Shields was opened.*

*A view of the first **Vega's** open bridge front. Seamen were exposed to the elements. On 16 November 1916 the **Vega** was sunk by a U-boat while on passage from Bergen to Newcastle. Fortunately everyone aboard was rescued and landed safely at Stavanger.*

Newcastle to her home port with a few passengers as well as freight. The result was disaster. On March 19 1917 the vessel suffered a torpedo attack and 18 people lost their lives, some of them dying in the lifeboats.

Another event in 1917, the year in which the Germans declared unrestricted submarine warfare, again proved just how dangerous crossing the North Sea could be. On December 12 the Fred Olsen steamer *Bollsta* was sunk by a flotilla of four German destroyers while sailing in convoy from the Tyne to Oslo with coal. Also sent to the bottom were five other merchant ships bound for various Scandinavian ports.

The convoy escorts were the British destroyers *Partridge* and *Pellew* and the armed trawlers *Livingstone*, *Commander Fullerton*, *Lord Alverstone* and *Tokio*. The *Partridge*, which had been completed by Swan Hunter and Wigham Richardson in 1916, and the armed trawlers were all sunk. Many men were killed or taken prisoner by the Germans, 97 being lost from the *Partridge*. The only ship to survive the attack was the *Pellew* which escaped in a rain squall. Some of the survivors, including merchant seamen, were picked up by British destroyers.

evade attack, reach Newcastle and return to Bergen safely, but after the sinking of the *Pollux*, a Bergen Line cargo ship, the situation was considered too dangerous to risk any other crossings. The *Venus* stayed in her home port for the rest of the war.

The *Pollux* had attempted the perilous crossing from

Other casualties of the war included the Northern Steamship Company's *Haakon VII*, which was damaged by an unknown submarine in the North Sea while carrying passengers and mail from Bergen to the Tyne. The Bergen Line's cargo vessel *Algol* simply disappeared in 1917 after leaving Newcastle for her home port. The Germans later stated that she was sunk by torpedo.

But enemy attack has never been the only danger which seamen face. On November 19 1916 the *Bessheim*, outward bound for Oslo, ran aground on the Black Middens rocks at the entrance to the Tyne. Severe gales had delayed the vessel's sailing.

A strong east south easterly gale was blowing as the *Bessheim* battled her way towards the piers at the river mouth. She was then hit by a mechanical problem and to observers on the shore the ship appeared to become unmanageable. It seems the vessel tried to turn around to return to safety but the wind blew her relentlessly towards the Black Middens, a notorious hazard to vessels entering or leaving the Tyne.

Bessheim grounded on the rocks and became helpless. The ship was carrying 87 passengers and 33 crew. But help was soon to arrive. The Tynemouth Volunteer Life Brigade went into action and a rocket was shot across to the vessel, two men being saved by breeches buoy.

Meanwhile, the Tyne's lifeboats had been launched. The National Lifeboat Institution's motor lifeboat *Henry Vernon* and the Tyne Lifeboat Society's *Tom Perry* and *Bedford* rescued the rest of the passengers and crew.

Later, when the weather moderated, the *Bessheim*'s cargo was removed by wherries (barges). The vessel was badly damaged on her starboard side, a hole in this area being given a temporary patch-up. On November 26 she was floated off on a flood tide with the help of the tugs *Royal Briton* and *Ulysses*. They towed the *Bessheim* to the Smiths Dock Company yard at North Shields where she was put into dry dock for repairs.

The *Bessheim* and the second *Stirling* continued in service after the First World War. The *Stirling* lasted until March 1922 when she was wrecked on a voyage to Newcastle while still in the Oslo Fjord. There were conflicting reports as to the cause. One account said she had hit a submarine, others that she had run aground.

Whatever, the reason, all the passengers and crew were saved and returned safely to Christiana. Two Britons had been aboard. A report stated that there was no panic. The *Stirling* sank in 78ft of water near the shore at Sandsen, close to Tvedestrand. The passengers' luggage sank with her.

Her replacement was the first *Blenheim*. All these vessels were equipped with triple expansion engines and ran on coal. *Bessheim* and *Blenheim* were faster than their predecessors and brought the Tyne-Oslo passage down to 42 hours. Passengers could now reach Norway's capital in under two days.

*Elegant lady. The Bergen Line's cruise ship **Stella Polaris** alongside the Tyne Commission Quay at its opening, 15 June 1928. Note the clipper-style bow.*

~ Trains to the Quay ~

At one time it was possible to travel from Bergen to the heart of Newcastle, landing on the city's Quayside after a voyage up the Tyne past the numerous shipyards and staiths.

The earliest ships on the passenger run to Bergen used the Albert Edward Dock, North Shields, as their departure and arrival point in the Tyne. However, in 1913 the Bergen ferries switched their berth to Newcastle Quayside which they used until the opening of the Tyne Commission Quay in 1928. They were then transferred to this new terminal.

From late 1921 the Bergen Line had found itself the sole operator of the Western Norway service after the Northern Steamship Company withdrew from the route.

Fred Olsen ships at first used Tyne Dock. Later, the company opened a berth at Newcastle Quayside which was used as well as the dock. Eventually, however, the Tyne Commission Quay would become the departure and arrival point for the Olsen vessels, sharing the facility with the Bergen Line.

The opening of the Tyne Commission Quay next to the Albert Edward Dock at North Shields in 1928 was a milestone in the history of the crossings to Norway. Through trains began operating direct from London via Newcastle to the quayside so that passengers could walk on to the ferries with little inconvenience and a considerable saving

*Right, the Bergen Line's first **Leda** at Newcastle Quayside in December 1920. The **Leda** was the first ship to sail from the newly completed Tyne Commission Quay, North Shields, in 1928.*

Newcastle Chronicle & Journal Ltd.

in time. From Bergen a railway service connected to Oslo. This sea and railway link became an increasingly important route for mail.

On June 15 1928 the chairman of the Tyne Improvement Commission officially opened the quay by unlocking the facility's transit shed with a golden key.

Moored alongside was the beautiful Bergen Line ship *Stella Polaris* which featured a clipper bow. The chairman of the commission and other guests were invited on board to inspect the vessel and given tea. Among those present was Bergen Line chairman Kristofer Lehmkuhl.

The *Stella Polaris* had been built for cruising, with the Norwegian fjords particularly in mind. She also went on world cruises during the winter months. Constructed by a Swedish yard, the elegant vessel offered luxurious accommodation and resembled a large-scale millionaire's motor yacht.

On the same day the Bergen Line ferry *Leda* began loading a cargo of 845 tons of coal and 155 tons of bunker coal at the quay in preparation for the first departure.

The following day the first direct boat train left London King's Cross at 9.30am bound for the quay. The train reached Newcastle Central Station at 3pm, and after a halt of about 15 minutes to take on more travellers, left the city for the waiting ships. A branch line from Percy Main ran right down to the quay.

The train arrived at the riverside at 3.50pm where, after the usual formalities, the passengers boarded the vessels. A local train from Newcastle arrived a little later with more people destined for Norway. Luggage was transferred to the two ships and the mails were loaded aboard the *Leda*.

Leda departed the quay at 5pm with 77 passengers for Bergen and the *Stella Polaris* half an hour later with 120 passengers who were being taken on a cruise.

The first ship to arrive with passengers at the new Tyne Commission Quay was the *Jupiter*, from Bergen, on June 17. She was carrying 41 passengers and a cargo of 139 tons of fish and 89 tons of general freight. Two of her holds were specially constructed to carry coal from the Tyne.

The *Jupiter*, built in Sweden, had first entered service on the run in 1916 but the following year was withdrawn because of the intensified U-boat campaign. From November 1917 she was chartered by the British government for a service between Bergen and Aberdeen and because of the wartime conditions was armed with a gun mounted aft.

After the First World War the *Jupiter* resumed service on the Newcastle run, remaining on the route until 1938. During one departure in the mid-1920s Tyne pilot Jack Walker, of North Shields, had guided the ship safely down river to sea but then encountered rough conditions as the vessel crossed the bar. He was unable to re-board the pilot boat, the danger being that he might be thrown into the water and crushed between the two vessels.

Jupiter's captain advised Jack to stay on board as a "passenger". The pilot thus had an unexpected trip to Bergen. On his arrival back in the Tyne he was presented with a coffee set by the Bergen Line as a souvenir of his surprise voyage. The coffee set bore the company's house flag logo and was used by Jack Walker's family for many years.

Jupiter went on to survive the Second World War and in 1946 returned to her old service, once again becoming a familiar sight in the Tyne with her tall funnel painted in the traditional Bergen Line black with silver horizontal stripes. She and the *Venus* of 1893 were the longest serving Bergen-Newcastle vessels.

Leda, the first ship to sail from the Tyne Commission Quay, was a sister of the *Jupiter*. She was built at Armstrong Whitworth's Low Walker Yard, Newcastle. The

Leda was launched into the Tyne at 4pm on May 4 1920 by the Lady Mayoress of Newcastle, Mrs Lee.

A little larger than the *Jupiter*, the ship had accommodation for 100 first and 47 third-class passengers. She was also fast, her geared turbine engines, constructed by the Wallsend Slipway & Engineering Company, giving her a speed of around 17 knots.

Mr K. Zimmer, of the Bergen Line, told guests at the launch that the company had lost 17 ships during the war and the *Leda* was the first replacement. Mr J.M Falkner, of Armstrong Whitworth, declared that the ship was one of seven vessels being built for Norwegian owners in the company's yards. The strong links between the North-East of England and Norway were once again in evidence.

Newcastle Chronicle & Journal Ltd.

*The first **Jupiter** approaches the Tyne Commission Quay. She was the first ship to arrive with passengers when the Quay was completed in 1928 and was carrying 41 passengers, 139 tons of fish and 89 tons of general freight.*

~ Rescue Ship ~

In 1931 a second *Venus* appeared at the Tyne Commission Quay. This handsome two-funnel ship had been built for the Bergen Line at the Elsinore Shipbuilding and Engineering Company's yard in Elsinore, Denmark. Powered by diesel engines, she was capable of up to 20 knots, making her the fastest vessel on the run. She could carry nearly 280 passengers.

The first *Venus*, by now a veteran of the North Sea, was renamed *Sylvia*, avoiding any confusion with the new vessel. The long-serving ship was withdrawn from the service in 1931.

The successful career of the second *Venus* plying between the Tyne and western Norway reached an extraordinary climax in January 1937 when storm force winds, rising to hurricane force at times, amid a blizzard turned the North Sea into an area of extreme danger.

As the *Venus* made her way from Bergen on passage to the Tyne she encountered formidable seas. Other, smaller ships were out there in the vast expanse, battling against the waves to reach the shelter of a port. These vessels included the Norwegian cargo carrier *Trym*, of Trondheim, with a crew of 19 aboard. Heavy seas crashed relentlessly on to the ship, badly flooding the galley and engine room. The crew realised she was in danger of sinking.

But help was to arrive. The wireless operator of the *Venus* picked up the *Trym*'s SOS call via a coastal radio station, and her master, Captain Wilhelm Dreyer, ordered his vessel to sail to the rescue.

When he reached the stricken ship's position, the cap-tain was unable to mount an immediate rescue attempt as night had fallen and the seas were too heavy. At one point the *Venus* even lost contact with the *Trym*, but eventually found her again.

The captain then called for volunteers to man a lifeboat. An attempt was to be made to save the *Trym*'s crew despite the appalling conditions. The response was overwhelming. Captain Dreyer found himself with too many volunteers. Only a handful of the *Venus*'s crew could be picked for a mission requiring great courage.

Amid the raging seas six men from the *Trym* were taken aboard the lifeboat and then returned to the rescue ship. This was made possible by the courage of *Trym* crew member Perry Opsahl who jumped into the water with a line and managed to reach the lifeboat. Five of his fellow crewmen were then brought to safety using a line and lifebuoy.

The youngest member of the *Trym*'s crew, 17-year-old Arne Ristan, was so exhausted he failed to grasp the lad-der after the lifeboat came alongside the *Venus*. Arne fell into the sea and was washed under the lifeboat. However, someone managed to catch hold of him and haul him to safety. Briefly unconscious, he awoke to find himself on the deck of the *Venus*.

But the operation was not yet over. Thirteen other men still remained on the *Trym* as she was pounded by the huge waves. However, luck was to change the situation. A temporary lessening of the storm provided the *Venus* with her opportunity. Displaying expert seamanship, Captain

Newcastle Chronicle & Journal Ltd.

*Safe arrival. The **Venus** arrives at the Tyne Commission Quay after the heroic rescue of the crew of the **Trym** in January 1937. A woman waves to the ship, and a photographer with a tripod captures the moment. Both the captain and crew members of the **Venus** were to receive awards for their humanitarian actions in the face of formidable seas.*

Dreyer brought his vessel close to the stricken steamer.

After several attempts, the *Venus* managed to shoot a line across to the *Trym* by means of a rocket and the remainder of the crew were hauled the short distance through the rough seas to the safety of the *Venus*'s decks by means of a line and lifebuoy.

This part of the operation took around two hours. The *Trym*'s men had been smashed against the sides of the ferry in the process, but all 19 were able to walk the deck of the rescue ship. Captain Torkildsen of the *Trym* was the last to leave his vessel.

The *Venus* pulled away from the sinking ship and sailed on towards the Tyne as she was violently assailed by the storm. The heavy seas smashed doors in the second-class compartments, causing flooding in one of the public rooms. Second-class passengers had to be moved to first-class accommodation after the water seeped into their cabins. Two crew members were slightly injured and a lifeboat was swept away amid the ferocity of the storm.

All aboard must have been greatly relieved as the *Venus* entered the sheltered waters between the Tyne piers, not least of them the 19 lucky men from the *Trym*. Captain Dreyer was moved by the warm welcome he and his crew received from the people of Tyneside upon landing.

He told the *North Mail*: "Watching the headquarters flag of the Tynemouth Volunteer Life Brigade dip in salute as we passed and seeing those hundreds of people gathered at the Commissioners' Quay I could not help but think to myself, 'so English'. We rescued Norwegians, but they treat us as though it had been Englishmen."

The *Venus*'s men had shown outstanding courage. Her captain had displayed fine seamanship, patience and perseverance in the face of exceptionally hazardous conditions.

King Haakon told members of the Norwegian parliament in Oslo: "I wish to express my thanks for this heroic deed, which shows the spirit of seamanship which still animates our able seamen in harmony with our best traditions."

For his key role in the rescue, Captain Dreyer was made a Knight Commander of Norway's Order of St Olav and received the Silver Medal of Lloyds of London. The seamen who manned the lifeboat were not forgotten either. They were awarded the Norwegian Gold Medal for a Noble Deed. Ordinary Seaman Perry Opsahl, from Aalesund, received the same honour for his outstanding bravery in taking the line to the lifeboat.

Tyneside had its own appropriate award for Captain Dreyer. He was made an honorary member of the Tynemouth Volunteer Life Brigade.

Newcastle Chronicle & Journal Ltd.

*A crowd welcome the **Venus** and relieved passengers stand on deck as the ship draws alongside at North Shields after the rescue. Among those aboard were the 19 members of the **Trym**'s crew saved from their sinking ship.*

~ Sunk and Salvaged ~

In June 1938 the second *Venus* was joined on the Bergen-Newcastle run by a beautiful new sister ship, the second *Vega*. Also sporting two funnels, the *Vega* was larger than her sister and could carry more than 450 passengers. She had been built in Trieste, Italy. However, the Second World War was to bring her career to a premature end.

The effects of that war were not long in showing themselves. The *Venus* and *Vega* were withdrawn from service because wartime insurance payments would have been far too high. However, the cargo service to and from Bergen was continued until the German invasion of Norway, and an old ship, *Mira*, made some passenger voyages.

The German invasion of Norway was to bring even these sailings to an end. *Mira* sailed from North Shields on April 29 1940 on course for Methil Roads in the Firth of Forth, arriving there on March 31. The following day she sailed for Bergen.

While still not far from the Scottish coast she was attacked by a squadron of German dive bombers. The Germans dropped five bombs, all of which missed the vessel.

Later, another two German aircraft flew over the *Mira*. Machine-gun fire rained down on her decks and two people were wounded. Then a British destroyer appeared on the scene and began firing at the planes. The *Mira* continued on her voyage while this battle was still in progress and reached Bergen without further mishap.

After landing, the relieved passengers praised the destroyer which had saved them. This warship is likely to have been from the Rosyth escort force, although her name was not reported at the time.

All passengers and crew of the *Mira* had survived, but the service was suspended from then onwards. The attack had taken place shortly before the Germans began their invasion of Norway.

Many of the company's ships were seized by the Germans, including the *Venus*, *Vega* and *Leda*. The elegant *Vega* was used by the Germans as a submarine depot vessel in the Baltic and in May 1945 was sunk by Allied bombers in Eckernfjord. It was a sad ending to a magnificent ship.

The single-funnel *Leda*, which had begun her life on the Tyne at Armstrong Whitworth's Low Walker Yard, was also seized. She too was eventually bombed and sent to the bottom by Allied aircraft near Stettin, Poland, in March 1945.

But the second *Venus* was to prove a lucky ship. The German navy used her as a depot vessel for U-boats, like the ill-fated *Vega*. As the war approached its closing stages in April 1945 she was bombed by Allied aircraft as she lay moored in Hamburg harbour and sank to the bottom.

However, the *Venus* was to be reborn. After the war, a salvage operation began and she was raised from the harbour bed. The ship was then towed from Hamburg to Denmark, where she underwent a major reconstruction. She emerged from this rebuilding with two new funnels and a new bow section. The *Venus* was now able to carry more than 400 passengers.

In 1948 the ship was placed back on the Bergen-Newcastle run. It was an extraordinary comeback. In winter she went on cruises to Madeira and Teneriffe, venturing far from the cold northern waters of her early years. The *Venus* now had a new lease of life, defying her previous misfortunes.

The *Jupiter*, which had begun her career during the First World War, also survived the Second Word War. She returned to the Newcastle run in 1946, becoming a veteran of the Tyne service. Operating mainly winter sailings while *Venus* went cruising, *Jupiter* was not withdrawn from the route until 1953-54.

She had her fair share of adventures. For example, in 1947 the ship strayed off course in dense fog as she approached the North-East coast. The first pilot boat she encountered was from the Wear instead of the Tyne. The Sunderland pilot boarded her and travelled in her to the Tyne, where the river's pilot boat put their man aboard. When the *Jupiter* berthed at Tyne Commission Quay onlookers witnessed the unusual sight of two pilots coming down the gangway.

The sturdy little ferry had given excellent service over many years. Before the Second World War, *Jupiter* carried Queen Maud of Norway on her trips to England and also took Prince Olaf and Princess Marthe back to their homeland after their honeymoon. Among her longest-serving masters were Captain T. Hansen and, later, Captain E. Lund.

In 1952-53 a new ferry was built for the Bergen Line's Tyne service at Swan Hunter & Wigham Richardson's Wallsend Yard. Launched by Princess Astrid of Norway in

Joyce Hall

*Remarkable survivor. The second **Venus** in the Tyne c.1960. Sunk during the Second World War, she was later salvaged, rebuilt, and placed back on the Newcastle-Bergen run.*

September 1952, she was named *Leda*, continuing the line's tradition of planet or star names. A beautifully proportioned vessel, she won great affection from both passengers and crew.

The new *Leda* was the first North Sea ferry to be equipped with stabilisers and she was also fast. Her turbine engines, built by the Wallsend Slipway & Engineering Company Ltd., gave her a normal service speed of 22 knots, but it was believed she could achieve up to 27. In 1954 the one-funnel ship reached Stavanger from the Tyne in a record 16 hours, 27 minutes. The direct run to Bergen took 19 hours. *Leda* thus reigned supreme as the North Sea speed queen.

Fred Olsen Line's **Black Watch** *alongside the company's berth at the Tyne Commission Quay on her maiden arrival in May 1938. Note the figurehead depicting a Highland soldier.* **Black Watch's** *sister, the* **Black Prince**, *had entered service earlier that year. Sadly, both ships were to be lost during the Second World War.*

~ Sisters From Oslo ~

Among the most beautiful of the Fred Olsen passenger ships to run on the Tyne-Oslo route were the 18-knot *Black Prince*, which began sailings in the summer of 1938, and her sister, the *Black Watch*, which entered service towards the end of the same year. They replaced the *Bessheim* and *Blenheim*. The new ships used the Tyne Commission Quay, their berth being situated by the side of the entrance to the Albert Edward Dock.

These vessels, driven by diesel engines, could make the crossing from North Shields to Kristiansand in 23 hours, reaching Oslo in 32. They were each able to carry 188 first-class and 68 second-class passengers.

The *Black Prince* sported a figurehead on her prow appropriately depicting England's Black Prince dressed in knight's armour. The *Black Watch's* figurehead was a Highland piper, a tribute to the famous Scottish regiment.

But like many other Norwegian ships, the two sisters became casualties of war. Their careers proved all too brief. In common with several of the Bergen Line vessels, they were used by the German navy as accommodation vessels during Hitler's occupation of Norway. The ships were seized in Oslo, where they had remained since the start of the war because of high insurance premiums.

The *Black Prince* was severely damaged during an allied bombing raid on Danzig, now known as Gdansk, in late 1942, and the *Black Watch* was sunk shortly before the end of the war in May 1945 by British naval aircraft. By then she had been pressed into service as a U-boat depot ship. It was an untimely ending for two superb Fred Olsen sisters.

After the war the Oslo service was re-launched using the *Bali* and the *Bretagne*. The *Bali* had formerly been the Tyne-Tees Steam Shipping Company's *Alnwick*, being com-

Newcastle Chronicle & Journal Ltd.

*The **Blenheim** at the Fred Olsen berth at Tyne Commission Quay. She was completed in 1951. Her career on the North Sea was ended by fire in 1968.*

pleted at Swan Hunter & Wigham Richardson's Neptune Yard in 1929. The *Bretagne* was completed by Akers Mek Verksted of Oslo in 1937.

However, these were only stop-gap ships. Fred Olsen wanted to replace the lost *Black Prince* and *Black Watch* with equally prestigious vessels. Accordingly, the company ordered two new ferries – both with aluminium alloy superstructures and hold space for about 40 cars. But they were in no sense roll-on, roll-off ships. The cars had to be lifted on and off by crane.

The first of these 16-knot sisters, built in Oslo, was the second *Blenheim*, completed in 1951. She sailed on her maiden voyage from Oslo to the Tyne in the spring of that year and was a stylish-looking ship which featured an unusual plastic glass-covered sun lounge behind her yellow aluminium-alloy funnel. This lounge, situated on the promenade deck, was dubbed the "Crystal Palace." It enabled travellers to sunbathe free from the chill of the cold North Sea winds.

Joyce Hall

The **Braemar**, the last of the old-style passenger ships on the Tyne-Norway services. Beginning her career in 1953, she did not retire until 1975 after 20 years on the Newcastle-Oslo run. The **Braemar** completed 1,300 round trips.

On her maiden voyage in 1951 the *Blenheim* carried 230 passengers, only seven short of her total capacity. She was decorated with carvings by Norwegian artists and one lounge featured a reconstruction of a living room in a typical Norwegian house.

The first cargo carried included 55 refrigerated one-tonne containers of snow. These were being sent to Edinburgh for a ski-jumping competition.

Among the passengers on board the *Blenheim* for her maiden voyage was Captain Fin Wickstrom. He com-

manded the *Bessheim* and *Black Prince* before the war and had spent many months helping to supervise the building of the *Blenheim*. The creation of the ship had been very much a joint venture between Britain and Norway. Her hull had been constructed by Thornycroft of Southampton and the rest of the ship was completed by Akers Mek Verksted of Oslo. It must have been a proud moment for Captain Wickstrom when the ship berthed at the Tyne Commission Quay.

Like many other vessels on the route, the *Blenheim*'s career was to have its dramatic moments. In March 1964 she limped into the Tyne 16 hours late after a 450-mile trip from Oslo with hatches battened down and passengers confined below decks. She had battled through 60ft waves in a fierce storm.

At times the ship was completely covered by the seas and her speed was greatly reduced. Most of the 108 British passengers were returning from skiing holidays in Norway. After the rough crossing, Captain Harald Muller found the piers of the Tyne a welcome sight.

But it was fire rather than a storm which eventually ended the *Blenheim*'s career upon the North Sea. In May 1968 she was hit by a blaze while outward bound from North Shields, 160 miles off the Norwegian coast. Fortunately her passengers and crew were safely rescued by fishing boats and helicopters. There were only two people injured. The following year the badly damaged vessel was sold and eventually became a car carrier.

The second of the two ships was the *Braemar*. She entered service in 1953 and proved herself to be an outstanding vessel, like her sister. The *Braemar*, of similar design to the *Blenheim*, did not retire until August 1975 after 22 years on the Tyne-Oslo run. She completed 1,300 round trips. Her figurehead depicted Braemar Castle in Scotland and like other names chosen in the past was clearly a tribute to Britain.

As she pulled away from the Tyne Commission Quay for the final voyage to Norway a Territorial Army band played *Auld Lang Syne* and Scottish pipers sounded a farewell.

People crowded the piers at Tynemouth and South Shields to wave goodbye to the elegant Norwegian mailboat. The *Braemar* was the last of the old-style passenger ferries on the Tyne-Norway crossings. It was now the era of the roll-on, roll-off ships built to accommodate large numbers of cars, lorries, vans and other motor vehicles as well as passengers. The old ships, however, were remembered with affection.

*Happy passengers on the gangway of the **Braemar** in the 1950s.*

~ The Ro-Ro Era ~

The debut of the roll-on, roll-off car ferries *Jupiter* and *Venus* in 1966 signalled the beginning of the end for the old-style passenger ships. The role of the old *Venus* on the route to Bergen was scaled down to winter weekend sailings and she was sent to the breaker's yard in Scotland in 1968. The speed queen *Leda* was withdrawn from the Tyne route in the autumn of 1974.

The car ferries *Jupiter* and *Venus* went on to prove highly successful and their ownership was shared between the Bergen and Fred Olsen lines. During the summer they sailed under their planetary names for Bergen Line but in winter they were sent on Fred Olsen cruises to the Canary Islands, the *Venus* becoming the *Black Prince* and the *Jupiter* the *Black Watch*.

Following the retirement of the *Braemar* in 1975, the car ferry *Borgen* maintained the Newcastle-Oslo service over the 1975-76 winter season. Afterwards, car ferries including the *Bolero* and a third *Blenheim*, sailed to Kristiansand, but did not run all the way to Oslo. However, in 1989-90 the second *Braemar*, a large car ferry, ran a Newcastle-Oslo service, briefly reviving the sea route to Norway's capital.

In 1981 the Danish company DFDS took over the operation of the *Venus* and *Jupiter*, although they were still owned by Bergen Line and Fred Olsen. However, in 1984 the Norway Line was formed, replacing the DFDS arrangement. This new line began sailings the following year, using the *Jupiter*.

Meanwhile, the *Venus* was chartered out to DFDS for their services from the Tyne. In 1986 she was withdrawn to be converted into a Fred Olsen cruise ship under her alternative name, *Black Prince*.

The *Jupiter* continued to be a familiar sight at the Tyne Commission Quay and in 1987 carried 71,000 passengers and about 10,000 vehicles. The sailing season was extended into December, enabling many Norwegians to do their Christmas shopping on Tyneside.

The year 1990 saw the *Jupiter* withdrawn from the route and a fourth *Venus* enter the Tyne to maintain the Bergen crossing. This car ferry had begun her career on Baltic sailings between Germany and Sweden under the name *Prinsessan Birgitta*.

Later in 1990 the Norway Line was replaced on the route by the Color Line which operated the service using at first the fourth *Venus* and later the *Color Viking* until 1998 when the Fjord Line took over. The *Color Viking* was renamed *Jupiter*, becoming the third ship of that name on the crossing.

Today, the Fjord Line's *Jupiter* maintains the service between the Tyne and western Norway, a sea crossing which has proved as enduring as the friendship between the two peoples.

*The car ferry **Jupiter** enters the Tyne in 1966. A new era had begun, sparked by the large increase in car ownership.*

~ A Life With The Ferries ~

David Robertson, of West Jesmond, Newcastle, worked for 50 years with the ferries, except for a four-year interval during the Second World War when he served with the Royal Navy. His employers for most of this time were P.H. Matthiesson, the Tyne agents for the Bergen and Fred Olsen lines. The firm had offices in Newcastle and at the Tyne Commission Quay.

Starting as an office boy on 10 shillings a week in October 1939, David rose to become passenger manager, working in this position for 25 years. He finished his career doing the same job with the Norway Line, before retiring in 1989.

Speaking of the first few months of the Second World War, he says: "As Norway was still neutral, there were still

Astrea at Bergen in 1947. She was one of the first ships to resume the Newcastle-Bergen run after the Second World War.

cargo vessels operating between the Tyne and Norway. My first job each morning was to telephone the office at Tyne Commission Quay to find out if any ships had arrived.

"This cargo service continued until April 6 1940 when the Germans invaded Norway. That day and the next we received hundreds of telegrams from firms asking us to cancel intended shipments. This was possible if consignments were still at the quay, but for ships en route to Norway nothing could be done until we heard what had happened to them. Some vessels were caught in Norway, but others managed to get back to Britain."

After his spell in the Navy, from 1942 until 1946, David returned to Matthiesson's. The *Lyra*, *Astrea* and *Jupiter* were the first Bergen Line ships back on the passenger route after the war. These vessels took many Norwegians home after their years of exile during the German occupation of their country. As usual, on some of these voyages scheduled calls were made at Stavanger and Haugesaund.

As well as passengers, the *Jupiter* and *Astrea* carried a wide variety of cargoes, including large amounts of fish. "The fish would be loaded aboard waiting trains and taken straight down to London to be sold at Billingsgate market. Sometimes the sailing times from Bergen would be changed to allow the fishing boats from the north of Norway more time to arrive in Bergen with their catches." Later, with the arrival of larger vessels, cargo ships docked at the quay carrying the fish.

In those first 10 years after the war the beautiful *Stella Polaris* helped out on the route to Bergen for a couple of summers. On one occasion a very thick fog enveloped the

Newcastle Chronicle & Journal Ltd.

*Speed queen. Dressed overall, the second **Leda** is seen here at the Tyne Commission Quay on her debut in 1953. She was launched by Princess Astrid at Swan Hunter and Wigham Richardson's Wallsend Yard in 1952, and went on to break speed records for the run to Western Norway.*

Tyne and David and his colleagues suddenly realised that the *Stella Polaris* had disappeared from her moorings, vanishing like a ghost into the murk.

"She sailed at 8pm, disappearing in almost an instant. We wondered whether she had made it safely out of the Tyne." The Lloyds hailing station was contacted, who told them the ship had left the river. They had not seen her but had heard her siren sounding through the fog.

David also remembers the *Bali* and *Bretagne* which were the first Fred Olsen ships back on the Oslo route after the war. "The *Bali* was a small vessel. She was commanded by a Captain Grimsgaard. He was succeeded by Captain Muller, who later commanded the *Blenheim*."

David recalls the 1950s when passenger traffic was flourishing: "In the mid-50s we had as many as 10 sailings each week – seven to Bergen and three to Oslo. Tyne Commission Quay on a Saturday had to be seen to be believed. *Venus* arrived from Bergen at 7am, followed by *Leda* at 11am.

"*Leda* sailed for Norway at 4pm, then *Braemar* to Oslo at 4.30pm (having arrived on Friday) and lastly *Venus* for *Bergen* at 5pm. We moved over 2,000 passengers practically every Saturday throughout the summer."

During one record year in the 1950s more than 130,000 travellers passed through the terminal.

David tells of the trains which took passengers right up to the quay: "In those days we had boat trains from King's Cross which was great for the passengers who simply boarded in London and got off at North Shields. The Tyne Commission Quay was a British Rail station. The most famous of the trains was named *The Norseman*. It was often full with passengers."

The name *The Norseman* was carried on a board across the front of the engine. David recalls there were stand-up menu cards depicting a Bergen Line funnel in the train's dining car.

"Of course, everything did not always go to schedule such as when the *Leda* came out of Bergen after an overhaul and got the blades of one turbine all nasty and twisted. It put her out of service for several weeks.

"This was at the beginning of the summer service so we were faced with many passengers booked and no ship. The main problem was for passengers with cars. For other travellers we chartered several airliners from Braathen and offered adjusted arrangements, including free hotel accommodation if necessary. I remember the first of these aircraft coming into Newcastle airport. It was, I think, a DC-8 which was the biggest plane ever to land there at the time."

The advent of the new roll-on, roll-off car ferries *Jupiter* and *Venus* in 1966 saw the end of the train service to the Tyne Commission Quay. The number of passengers travelling by rail was declining. The opening of a new terminal hundreds of yards away from the railway line was another problem which contributed to the decision to withdraw the trains.

David explains: "Because of the size of these ships and the fact that cars could be driven on and off, as against crane loading which had been necessary with all previous vessels, we had to build a new terminal at the quay. Unfortunately, this was away from the railway line which meant that we could no longer use trains. Passengers could still travel by train to Newcastle but would have to transfer to buses to take them to the quay.

"In addition, more and more people were travelling by car, so this reduced the number requiring public transport. In fact, British Rail had already been on to us with a proposal to stop using the boat trains because fewer passengers were using them."

David says the worst disaster during his time with the ferries was the blaze aboard the *Blenheim* while en route to Oslo in 1968. "She sailed from the Tyne on a Tuesday and

*A bird's eye view of the ro-ro terminal at the Tyne Commission Quay, North Shields, c.1970. The **Jupiter** is alongside. The Albert Edward Dock can be seen top right.*

the fire began on Wednesday morning. Fortunately all passengers and crew were saved, but it meant that instead of three sailings each week we were reduced to three each fortnight.

"At the beginning of the summer, and unable to find a suitable passenger vessel to take her place, this gave us problems – more or less what had happened with the *Leda*. Again, we used aircraft where possible."

The routes to Norway were used by a considerable number of celebrities over the years. David remembers that the comic film star Will Hay was a regular traveller. On one occasion Will's Daimler was unloaded at the quay by crane and the next car to be lifted off came crashing down on top of it. The chain had snapped. "Will was really very good about it and simply said 'Well bless my soul' – just as he would have done on the screen."

Other celebrities included Peter Scott, the television naturalist, and H.S.H. Guinness, a member of the famous brewing family. "Mr Guinness was a keen angler who went to Norway for the fishing."

David made many Norwegian friends during his career and went to evening classes for a year to learn the country's language.

In his last years at the quay he worked with Dag Romslo, who was UK director of the British section of Norway Line. Dag now heads the UK operation of the Fjord Line. His father, Malvin Romslo, was a founder of Norway Line and also held leading posts at various times with Fred Olsen and Bergen Line, as well as working for Norwegian State Railways in earlier years.

When David Robertson retired in 1989 a party was held for him aboard the car ferry *Jupiter* as she lay alongside the Tyne Commission Quay. David was surprised when the Norwegian Consul Nigel Westwood stood up and read out a fax from the Norwegian Embassy in London.

David Robertson, right, is presented with a bottle of champagne by Norwegian Consul Nigel Westwood aboard the car ferry **Jupiter** *on his retirement in 1989.*

The fax said that David had been awarded Norway's prestigious St Olav's Medal for his "exceptional contribution to the fostering of the friendship across the North Sea" over 50 years. He was then presented with a large bottle of champagne from the consulate.

A week later, at the Norway Line's Christmas party, also aboard the *Jupiter*, Nigel Westwood presented him with the medal. It was a wonderful ending to his long career with the ferries.

~ Fondly Remembered Ships ~

People on Tyneside speak of the Norway ferries with great affection. They were always known as the "mailboats". Indeed, until aircraft took over the job of carrying letters and packages, these ships were a vital link in the postal system between Britain and Norway.

The ferries have been a familiar sight to all who live close to the mouth of the Tyne. When you talk to people who feel affection for these ships, their memories come flooding back. A considerable number of Norwegians live on Tyneside and there are Tynesiders who have family connections with the land of the fjords.

Every year, the city of Bergen sends a large Christmas tree to its "twin" city of Newcastle as a thank-you present for the help Tyneside people gave to the Norwegians during the Second World War. Adorned with traditional silver lights, it is placed outside Newcastle Civic Centre, a symbol of friendship and affinity.

Joyce Hall, of Tynemouth, describes herself as a "devotee of Norway". She was born in Edinburgh but has lived by the Tyne since she was aged six. As a girl before the Second World War she and her friends would often walk to the end of Tynemouth Pier at night and stand beneath the lighthouse beam to see her favourite ship, the second *Venus*, depart the river.

Joyce also sometimes attended the Norwegian church which was attached to the Seamen's Mission in Borough Road, North Shields, and remembers the crews from the ferries worshipping there.

She became fascinated by Norway, its culture and Norse mythology. After the Second World War Joyce learned Norwegian, taking lessons from a student teacher, Leif Gjerlow, who had come to Britain to perfect his English. "The Geordie dialect is very much related to Norwegian," she declares.

In 1947, Joyce fulfilled a long-held ambition to travel to the land of the fjords and booked a trip aboard the *Astrea*, one of the first ships back on the Bergen route after the war. Among the places she visited was the magnificent Sognefjord.

The following year she again made the voyage in *Astrea*, and in later years travelled six more times to Norway. In 1969, for example, she sailed in the *Braemar* to Oslo. Joyce has photograph albums full of pictures which reveal her delight in those holidays, some of which she

Devotee of Norway. Joyce Hall, from Tynemouth, by one of the lakes at Bergen. A welcome holiday after the tensions of wartime.

enjoyed with her husband. They also contain a lovingly preserved cabin card and luggage label.

She made a considerable number of friends during her travels. Joyce recalls meeting two American servicemen on board the *Astrea* who were "horrified" at the stringency of the post-war rationing endured by Britons. Afterwards they sent her a tin of cooking fat known as "Spry" as a present. "They nicknamed me Spry Joyce," she says, with a broad smile.

The ordeals of the wartime occupation of Norway were still fresh in people's memories at this time. Joyce recorded in her diary that she and Leif walked past the U-boat pens at Bergen and saw the damage done by RAF bombs to these concrete structures, built to protect the submarines.

She wrote: "Further on we came to the local cemetery and saw the well kept graves of the victims of those raids. Pitiful, but these things cannot be helped if wars are to be won. Unfortunately a school had been hit – poor, innocent children." Leif had been a student teacher at the school.

Joyce is a painter and as an artist has an eye for the beauty of a finely lined ship. "The *Venus* was one of the

*On the way home to the Tyne, 1947. Passengers aboard **Astrea** lounge in deckchairs enjoying the sea air.*

most photogenic ships I have ever seen. The vessel looked wonderful in her black and silver livery. However, I remember sailing back from Bergen on one occasion and finding her painted yellow and white (her cruising colours) and I didn't like it."

Joyce does not confine her passion to just one ship, however. She remembers with affection many of the other vessels and attended the launch of the second *Leda* by Princess Astrid at Wallsend in 1952. Astrid had arrived at North Shields aboard the *Venus* and was accompanied by Crown Prince Olaf and her sister, Princess Ragnhild.

Joe Addison, of South Shields, served as a deckhand in steam tugs on the Tyne from 1947 until 1951, working for the tug firms Ridley and France, Fenwick.

Joe helped bring the Norway boats in and out of the river on many occasions. Two tugs were needed each time, one forward and one aft. He served in several of these sturdy little vessels, including the *Marty*, *Monty*, *Corsair* and *Washington*.

Later in his life he had the pleasure of sailing to Norway as a passenger nine times, on one occasion taking his grandsons. "The voyages were beautiful. They were good for the soul. I liked sailing through the calm waters of the fjords."

Olga Carlson, of South Shields, is one of the many people living by the Tyne who has strong connections with the ships. Her father was Norwegian and worked as a "checker" supervising the loading and unloading of cargoes for Fred Olsen at the Tyne Commission Quay. He was employed in this job from the 1920s until the outbreak of war in 1939. After the conflict, he returned to the quay and did the same job.

His name was Otto Hagemann, and he came originally from Trondheim. Otto had served in sailing ships before taking up his shore job.

Olga recalls that every morning her father would leave their home in Canterbury Street and walk all the way to the South Shields ferry terminal, cross to North Shields and then walk to the Tyne Commission Quay to start work.

He was employed as a checker for many years after the war until his retirement following an accident. A pit prop dropped on his foot while he was down a hold. Otto was treated at the Ingham Infirmary, South Shields. "It was only then that Matthiesson's found out his age. He was 81," says Olga. "They told him he was far too old to continue working."

Martin Melling, of Cleadon, South Tyneside, also has close ties with the ferries. His father was Norwegian and his mother English. The couple met in Liverpool during the Second World War while his father was serving in the North Atlantic convoys as a ship's carpenter in merchant vessels.

After the war they decided to settle in Norway, sailing in 1947 in the second *Venus* to Bergen. Martin was 18

Olga Carlson

Otto Hagemann, from Trondheim, who worked as a checker at the Tyne Commission Quay for many years.

months old at the time. They lived for a while in the village of Meling, from which his family take their name, on the island of Bømlo, south of Bergen at the mouth of the Hardanger Fjord. However, they later moved to Oslo.

In 1949 they sailed back to North-East England aboard the *Bali*, settling in North Shields, where Martin was brought up. Over the years since then he has often visited relations in Norway and sailed in the sister ships *Blenheim* and *Braemar*. "These two ships would dip their ensigns and sound their horns when they passed each other in the North Sea."

Joan Phillips, of Cullercoats, speaks of the second *Venus*, the famous rescue ship, with great enthusiasm and affection. While in her 20s, she often saw the vessel entering and departing the Tyne. "I fell in love with the *Venus*. The ship was a beautiful sight and it would lift your spirits." Joan travelled to Norway on the *Venus* twice and learned Norwegian, so great was her enthusiasm for the country, its people and ships.

Joan had an aunt and uncle who lived in Promontory Terrace by the seafront in Cullercoats. She remembers visiting her cousin Betty who played the piano and first seeing the second *Venus*. She writes: "Cousin Betty was a fine pianist with a light, feathery voice to match. It was in a large room facing the sea during one of her little recitals that I had my first sighting of the Norwegian mailboat en route from the Tyne to her home port.

"Something about her stirred my romantic imagination and ever after I was a fervent ship watcher, with the *Venus* at the top of my list. This vessel sailed regularly from the Tyne, and Cullercoats people made a habit of standing on the Bank Top on Saturday afternoons to watch her pass the piers, checking their watches to see if she was on time.

"A few of us would often walk along Tynemouth Pier just for the pleasure of that magic moment when the *Venus* slowly rounded the bend in the river, then gathered speed to cross the bar. She was a beautiful sight to see, her prow moving forward like the proverbial swan in the evening over the lake.

"Sometimes she brought King Haakon and Queen

*The second **Leda** leaves the Tyne. A Stephenson Clarke 'flat iron' collier is seen to her left, inbound.*

Maud to Britain – they often took a walk along the seafront at Tynemouth for exercise before going south to London.

"The good ship *Venus* continued her crossings for many a year and I can recall being on the Fish Quay at North Shields when she called in after rescuing some local fishermen. Everyone lined up alongside the quayside to give captain and crew a rousing reception."

Those who worked with the ferries also have their fond memories of them. Mike Shipley, of Newbiggin-by-the-Sea, Northumberland, served as a barman on the car ferry *Jupiter* in 1966-67 and he describes her as "one of the happiest ships I've ever worked in".

"There were only three Britons working on board at the time – myself, the drummer and the organist – but the crew consisted of 27 different nationalities. The countries represented included Austria, Italy, New Zealand, Australia, France and Germany. Most of the officers were

Norwegian." Mike had a few rough crossings but they do not seem to have worried him. "We enjoyed the rough voyages. It was easier because fewer passengers surfaced."

Pat Fawcett, of Whitley Bay, worked as a cleaner aboard the vessels at Tyne Commission Quay from 1972 to 1975. "My favourite ship was the *Braemar*. She was wonderful. The woodwork was lovely."

Pat remembers that one captain made a point of checking on the number of coat hangers left in each cabin after cleaning. "He was very particular about this, insisting that five were always left."

Alan Chaplin, of Wallsend, was employed at the quay in 1953-54. He writes: "I commenced work on April 7 1953 for P.H. Matthiesson as an office boy, aged 15. This was the day on which the second *Leda* made her maiden voyage from the Tyne. Before the vessel sailed on this very warm spring day a large party was held on deck." Alan praises the hospitality of captain and crew and the wonderful food that was served to guests on such occasions. Besides

*Rough weather in the North Sea seen from the deck of the second **Leda**, November 1971.*

the maiden Tyne departure of the *Leda*, he also remembers a party being held on the *Bretagne* before her last voyage from the Tyne.

"The passenger lounge for the Bergen Line was quite lavish and most impressive to passengers by the standards of the 1950s. Comparatively few cars were shipped at that time and most passengers either arrived or left the Tyne Commission Quay by train.

"In addition to a great deal of general cargo being handled, a large amount of fish was imported, including dried fish sewn into hessian sacking."

Alan tells of a dramatic moment at the quayside station: "When going to the Bergen shed from Matthiesson's office the more agile of us crossed the road and jumped up on to the platform where the trains arrived.

"On one occasion a new employee had seen us doing this and decided to follow suit. Unfortunately, he failed miserably, one leg landing on the platform at right angles to the other which was just managing to touch the track at the side of the platform. Unable to get either up or down from the platform he was eventually pulled to safety by a quick-thinking baggage handler with an incoming train just 15-20 yards away."

Nick Robinson, of Seaton Sluice, has a family connection with the ships. His father, Colin, was chief engineer of the car ferry *Blenheim*, which did runs between the Tyne and Kristiansand and sometimes to Bergen in the late 1970s and early 1980s.

Nick has sailed to Norway several times himself and visited the offices of Fred Olsen in Oslo. "There was a war memorial plaque in the foyer on which were recorded the names of the Fred Olsen seamen who lost their lives during the Second World War," he says, adding that one man was listed as being killed by the Gestapo.

Dick Keys

~ Voyagers' Tales ~

In the 1950s and 60s, Michael Irwin, of Gosforth, Newcastle, was a regular visitor to Norway from the Tyne. His business was selling coal and coke and buying Norwegian steel.

Michael tells of an encounter which left him feeling distinctly chilled: "I well recall a voyage in Fred Olsen's *Blenheim*. It was late at night in the lounge and I was drinking with a Norwegian. He suddenly told me that he was a 'murderer'.

"He said he had worked at a printing company during the Second World War which produced illegal propaganda for the resistance movement against the Germans.

"One day the Gestapo raided their premises and the staff, including himself, were arrested. They were sent to a camp near Oslo and a number of them were then sent to German concentration camps. Some died in Germany.

"On his return to Oslo my drinking friend found out that one of the staff had betrayed them to the Germans. The man was a collaborator.

"The collaborator disappeared after the war until one summer's night my friend stopped for an ice cream in an alleyway off a main street in Oslo. The seller was the man who had betrayed them.

"My friend said that in darkness he murdered the collaborator and threw his body into the Oslofjord. I never forgot that crossing of the North Sea."

Tales concerning the Norway ferries are not always, of course, so harrowing or grim. Those taking holidays generally have fond memories of their trips.

For example, in August 1952, John Winterburn, who was living at the time in Gateshead, sailed to Norway aboard the first *Jupiter*. He remembers that he and two other young men slept in bunks grouped around the forehold. They were travelling under the auspices of the Youth Hostels Association and the fare from North Shields to Bergen cost £10 return.

He writes: "We were three in number going for a walking holiday in the Jotenheim Mountains. We took the boat train from the Central Station, Newcastle, to the ferry terminal on August 18 1952. The return fare to Norway should have cost £12 but as members of the YHA we were

Passengers sleep or simply relax aboard the first **Jupiter** *in 1952.*

entitled to a £2 discount.

"After boarding *Jupiter*, we were directed to the dormitory accommodation in the fo'c'sle. Access was directly from the deck, the beds (or bunks) were arranged between the hull and the wooden partitioning surrounding the forward hold. The forward end of the dormitory was of steel plate and, presumably, the chain locker lay beyond.

"There was not much light, either natural or artificial, no specific seating area and two toilets with washbasins for the 30 or so passengers in that area.

"We ate in the only dining room after the first two sittings for the second-class passengers. The food was good as we chose from the same menu.

"We had clear skies and a fresh breeze, with the sea running a typical North Sea chop. There were chairs around the main hold in front of the bridge, first priority being given to second-class, and we stretched on top of the hold. However, as soon as the second-class passengers were called for a meal there was a rush to bag one of the vacated chairs.

"First port of call was Stavanger where we docked at night. Loud noises in the middle of the night came from the forward hold around which we were trying to sleep – very loud noises!

"The following day, after breakfast, all passengers were invited to join a bus tour of Stavanger. The cost was minimal. At one stop we were taken around a recently completed hotel with polished wooden floors. We offered to take off our hobnailed boots but were told not to bother!

"We arrived at Bergen the same day. Our most important document was a timetable which included all countrywide services for road, rail and sea. Perhaps it is still produced. We had time to buy some provisions before catching the small coastal ferry to Laerdal on the Sognefjord.

"It was a great holiday. This included climbing Glittertind (the highest point but not the highest mountain in Northern Europe), teaching and dancing Strip the Willow (in stocking feet and to the music of a Norwegian polka) and helping to push our bus out of snow drifts on the Sognefjell. We returned, of course, on the *Jupiter*, leaving Bergen at 2pm on the 30th."

Kari Thúróczy, of Oslo, made the voyage from Norway to Tyneside in the summer of 1954 when she was aged 17. Kari writes: "How my friend Irene and I were allowed by our parents to go hitch-hiking in England for three weeks I don't know. I was 17 and Irene 16. But maybe they thought England was a 'safe' place with kind and friendly people. And they were right!

"We sailed on the ferry from Oslo to Newcastle. The sea was very rough. Most of the passengers got seasick, but I and a few whalers enjoyed the meals. Irene did not leave our cabin.

"We met so many nice, kind and charming people. Three happy weeks with much laughter, but not much money.

"The day before our home journey we didn't have a penny left. But we had bought tickets in advance for the ferry from Newcastle to Bergen and from there the train to Oslo.

"But on the day of departure the people at the quay told us that the ferry was full and that we might not get back to Norway on that day. And they asked us a lot of questions about our journey. We didn't understand they were teasing us. We were the last passengers to board the ship.

"We didn't get a cabin, so we had to stay awake till all the passengers had gone to bed. The crew members were very kind. They brought us food and juice and pillows. We slept on sofas in a lounge."

Many years later Kari met and fell in love with Peder Magne Klepsvick, a Norwegian wartime hero. As a young man Peder and a friend escaped from German occupied Norway in a rowing boat with a small sail and made the perilous voyage from the island of Indoy to Scotland. He joined the Norwegian Merchant Navy in exile and then Britain's Royal Air Force. In later years Peder served in the Norwegian Air Force and rose to the rank of lieutenant colonel. He died in 2001.

Rigmor Grimsø, of Husøysund, tells two stories of the Oslo crossing. She writes: "As we have close relatives in Great Britain, my parents quite often crossed the North Sea on one or other of Fred Olsen's ships from Oslo. It was a comfortable way of travelling and – provided the sea was not too rough – the sumptuous meals on board were quite a treat.

"On one of their crossings they met a female fellow passenger, with whom they had many a pleasant conversation. However, always at meal times, when they asked if she would join them for the meal she excused herself and went to her cabin.

"Just at the very end of the voyage they discovered that she had brought her own food in order to save money. She didn't know that when travelling from Oslo the meals were always included in the ticket! Quite a sad story really!"

NEWCASTLE - OSLO

CONNECTIONS BY BRITISH RAILWAYS		All departures 2/5–13/6 and after 4/9	All departures 15/6—4/9	Local Train	
London (King's X)	dep.	9.00 A	9.30 A	Sats 9/5-13/6 Weds 27/5 3/6, 10/6 Mon 8/6	15/6-5/9
Newcastle Central	arr.	13.48	14.05		
Newcastle Central	dep.	14.04	14.10	13.30	13.45
Newcastle T.C.Q.*	arr.	14.39	14.48	14.05	14.20

		2—23/5 & 29/9		25/5—26/9	
Newcastle (T.C.Q.*)	dep.	Tues., Sat.	4.30pm	Mon., Wed., Sat.	4.30pm
Kristiansand	arr.	Wed., Sun.	5.00pm	Thurs., Sun	5.00pm
Kristiansand	dep.		5.30pm		5.30pm
Oslo (Vippetangen)	arr.	Thurs., Mon	7.00am	Wed., Fri., Mon.	7.00am

Summer Rail Services 31/5 — 19/9

		✕	☕	⇔✕	✕		✕	☕	✕	☕	✕
Oslo	dep.	9.10	13.05		9.10	9.10	9.50	13.50	8.45	12.35	10.05
Trondheim	arr.	20.20	21.08 →	21.45							
Bodø	arr.			10.45							
Åndalsnes	arr.				18.35						
Fagernes	arr.					14.00					
Bergen	arr.						19.40	21.45			
Gothenburg	arr.								13.20	16.56	
Stockholm	arr.										F 18.00

Rigmor adds: "I suppose none of us were especially modest when it came to digging into the great variety of courses served at the lunch table on board, but some people obviously were even less so than others. On one of my parents' crossings they observed a woman reproaching one of the other passengers for helping himself from her plate. 'Oh, I'm so sorry,' he replied, 'I only helped myself from the plate where I found the most!'"

Martin Melling, of Cleadon, South Tyneside, writes of the ferries: "My first memory of these ships was of the *Bali*. She was an old, three-castle, coal-fired steamship. Even in 1950 she was beginning to become old fashioned. It was the dawn of the dominance of the motor vessel.

"My Norwegian father, Ole Melling, was a ship's carpenter on the *Bali*. I was on board, not quite sure why, just before sailing. I had clearly been told to stay put in his cabin while the vessel shifted ship to take bunkers.

"The view from the porthole was fascinating as the ship was warped along to the coal staiths. The noises were incredible. The clang of heavy metal on metal, the grinding of the ship's side against the quay, the rattle and squealing of the coal trucks, the crashing of the coal as it tumbled into the bowels of the ship and the distant shouting of men's voices.

"When I look back on it now it was an incredible experience for a boy of five, but then as the only son of a Norwegian seafarer father and English mother I had an amazingly rich childhood. My whole life is interlaced with experiences and memories of the Fred Olsen and Bergen Line ships and, of course, latterly the Color Line and Fjord Line. Being half Norwegian I have strong family bonds and affinities with Norway that draw me back across the North Sea time and time again.

"As a young boy I would often accompany my mother, either to North Shields Fish Quay or Tynemouth Pier to wave to my father as he sailed out of the Tyne for Oslo. I

The sumptuous cold table, from Fred Olsen's brochure for Summer, 1964.

those days the turn around was much slower and he would be away for five days.

"My father was a very quiet and shy man, and was not a great one for telling tales of derring-do. However, occasionally, encouraged by friends and relatives and usually when he had a few drinks aboard, he would recount seafaring experiences.

"One such tale was of the storm of 1953. He was serving as carpenter on the *Blenheim*. I think it may have been late January or early February. The weather forecast was very bad and there were predictions of winds in excess of storm force 10 in the North Sea. The captain decided to delay departure. However, about an hour later the *Leda* set sail for Bergen. The captain of the *Blenheim* also decided to sail and the vessel was prepared for sea.

"Within minutes of leaving the Tyne she was being battered and buffeted by very heavy seas. My father had been battening down internal porthole covers but had not finished before he was called away to attend to other matters on deck. Eventually the *Blenheim* was shipping so much green water that all hands were called below decks. The scene there was chaos. The motion of the ship was so violent that anything loose was being hurled from one side to the other. The galley became unusable for many hours. Not that it mattered much, since many passengers were seasick in their cabins.

"Things became even worse the next morning and the vessel was virtually 'hove to' for many hours riding out the worst of the storm. I seem to recall that when she finally limped into Oslo she was 24 hours behind schedule. Several of the crew had been injured and much damage sustained."

Joyce Hall, of Tynemouth, tells of a particularly rough passage home in the *Astrea* in 1948. She wrote in the diary she kept of the trip: "There was cold meat with salad and stew and mashed potatoes for lunch, and I ventured out on deck again, but it began to rain.

"Quite a bad storm got up, and it was impossible to walk about or sit in any comfort as the *Astrea* was rolling and pitching so badly. Water was coming in through the toilets and the washbasins and corridor were awash. I was afraid of being seasick so I lay down in my bunk – it was the best place anyhow. But I weathered it OK.

"We reached the Tyne at 2am and I awoke immediately as I felt the easing of the motion. I rose at 6am and had ham omelette and cold meat for breakfast at 6.30 – I was ravenous! … I was ashore at 7.30am."

Ann Jobling, (née White) of South Shields, has been travelling back and forwards to Oslo since 1951. Her first trip was by aircraft from Newcastle as one of 30 schoolchildren from Sunderland and South Shields who were going to stay with Norwegian families as a "thank you" to the people of the North-East who looked after Norwegian seamen and others during the Second World War. Ann made close and lasting friendships on that trip.

Later, she travelled on the *Braemar* and *Blenheim*, and describes the experience as "pure luxury". She comments: "Even though I was a second-class passenger accommodation and food were marvellous. Can you imagine a 16-year-old's eyes when I first saw the smorgasbord table after the war years?"

In 1971 Ann crossed to Oslo with her husband and small son. "He dropped his toy car over the side and was ready to jump in after it! I remember the crossing was a little rough – enough for a little boy to be seasick."

Another voyage, in 1975, was made in the *Borgen*. "That was quite a trip as there was a technical problem and we were delayed in Kristiansand until a replacement could be organised."

Ann remembers a crossing in late September 1980 which she describes as "terrible". "My two young daughters and myself were again travelling to visit our friends in Oslo. The crossing out wasn't too bad, but the trip home was awful. We had all taken our anti-seasickness pills as we had been warned it was going to be bad.

"We had a little supper and went to our cabin. The seas were so

Ann Jobling enjoying Norwegian hospitality.

Ann Jobling

Newcastle Chronicle and Journal Ltd.

*In this atmospheric picture foyboatmen secure the second **Jupiter** on arrival at the Tyne Commission Quay in 1984.*

rough my youngest daughter, who was aged eight at the time, was literally thrown from one end of the bunk to the other. It was dreadful. The seas were hitting the bow of the ship as if we were hitting rocks. The girls were petrified and I wasn't too happy myself.

"We did get to sleep eventually, and then I was woken by alarm bells ringing and the captain telling everyone to go to their lifeboat stations. The girls got some warm clothes. I quickly dressed as well and we got up on deck to find some of the ship's crew playing the one-armed bandits etc. Then I realised I had had a nightmare. It was just a bad dream, thank goodness. Believe me, I could do without dreams like that."

Ann still travels to Oslo every year to stay with friends she has made, although these days she goes by air. "Unfortunately, the gentleman I stayed with originally, from 1951, has now died. His wife passed away 14 years before him. They are a big miss in my life as they had no children and spoiled me and mine for 49 years. They were part of my family."

Ann's words are moving testimony to the friendship between the peoples of North-East England and Norway, an enduring relationship in which the ferries have played a leading role.

The Fjord Line's **Jupiter**, *the third Tyne-Norway ferry to bear the name, enters the Tyne in 2000.*

A NORWAY FERRIES CHRONOLOGY

1865 The *Nordland* sails on the first officially advertised passenger steamship service from Newcastle to Norway (Trondheim).

1868 The *Saga* begins a summer service between Newcastle and Bergen.

1890 A passenger and mail service begins between Trondheim, Bergen and Newcastle. The service is shared between Bergen Steamship Company (Bergen Line), the Northern Steamship Company of Trondheim and P.G. Halvorsen. East Norway Lloyd line begins passenger ship service between Newcastle and Christiania (Oslo).

1906 Fred Olsen Line takes over the Newcastle-Oslo service from East Norway Lloyd.

1916 Bergen Line's first *Vega* sunk by U-boat in North Sea. Passengers and crew saved.

1928 Tyne Commission Quay (also known as the Riverside Quay) is opened.

1937 Bergen Line's second *Venus* rescues 19 crew of cargo ship *Trym* during fierce storm.

1939-45 Second World War. Bergen Line's second *Vega*, first *Leda*, and Fred Olsen's *Black Watch* and *Black Prince* lost as a result of conflict. The second *Venus* sunk, but later salvaged and reconstructed. The first *Jupiter* also survives.

1954 Bergen Line's second *Leda* sets a record by reaching Stavanger from the Tyne in 16 hours 27 minutes. She reduces direct run to Bergen to 19 hours.

1966 Car ferries *Venus* and *Jupiter* introduced on Newcastle-Stavanger-Bergen service.

1975 Fred Olsen's first *Braemar* withdrawn, the last of the old-style passenger ships.